No .... Class ....557...........

Author ...STEELE Philip...........................

Title ...Storms...

WEATHER WATCH

Storms
CAUSES AND EFFECTS

Philip Steele

Franklin Watts
London   New York   Sydney   Toronto

© 1991 Zoe Books Limited

Devised and produced by
Zoe Books Limited
15 Worthy Lane
Winchester
Hampshire SO23 7AB
England

First published in 1991
in Great Britain by
Franklin Watts Ltd
96 Leonard Street
London EC2A 4RH

First published in Australia by
Franklin Watts Australia
14 Mars Road
Lane Cove
New South Wales 2066

ISBN 0 7496 0457 3

A CIP catalogue record for this book is available from the British Library.

Printed in the United Kingdom

Design: Jan Sterling
Picture researcher: Jennifer Johnson
Illustrators: Tony Kenyon, Gecko Ltd.

Photographic acknowledgements
Cover: (centre) Tony Stone Worldwide, (outer) Paul Berger / Tony Stone Worldwide.
p1 Heather Angel, p3 V Streano / ZEFA Picture Library, p4 Tony Stone Worldwide, p5 D Simson / Barnaby's Picture Library, p6 J Hartley / Panos Pictures, p7 Geoff Moon / Frank Lane Picture Library, p9 D Hoadley / Frank Lane Picture Library, p10 R P Lawrence / Frank Lane Picture Library, p11 J Hartley / Panos Pictures, p13 Gordon Garradd / Science Photo Library, p15 J Allen Cash Ltd, p16 Mary Evans Picture Library, p17 Richard Packwood / Oxford Scientific Films, p 18 NASA / Science Photo Library, p19 Robert Harding Picture Library, p20 B Klass / Panos Pictures, p21 L Campbell / NHPA, p22 Barnaby's Picture Library, p23 D Hollands / Frank Lane Picture Library, p24 Trygve Bølstad / Panos Pictures, p25 J Allen Cash Ltd, p26 Popperfoto, p27 ZEFA Picture Library, p28 Dr D Booth / Geo Science Features, p29 J Hartley / Panos Pictures.

Contents

Storm warning

◀ Lightning forks across the sky linking the clouds and land with a massive electrical charge.

Storm gods

Storms are dangerous. Long ago, people thought that they were the work of gods in the sky. The ancient Greeks believed in a storm god called Typhon, who unleashed terrible monsters to wreck ships and drown sailors.

In Germany and Scandinavia, people used to believe that storms were caused by the ghosts of dead warriors, riding across the sky in a battle-rage. One Scandinavian god was called Thor. He was the god of thunder, and it was the noise of his hammering that was heard on the Earth below. Thor struck down his enemies with lightning.

▶ Storm force winds can be very destructive in cities. They can blow down advertising hoardings and scaffoldings, as well as causing damage to buildings.

The first signs of any storm can be exciting. The wind rises, blowing leaves along the street, and heavy rain drums on the roof. Thunder rumbles in the distance.

However, when the full force of a bad storm strikes, it may be terrifying. Sometimes trees are uprooted, buildings damaged and towns flooded. Farms can be cut off by snow and roads blocked.

Each year, disasters around the world show that although humans may be able to travel through space and walk on the Moon, they still cannot control the weather. As recently as November 1970, a storm in Bangladesh flooded farmland and washed away homes, killing about one million people.

What is a storm?

The word "storm" is used to describe any violent disturbance in the **atmosphere**. It can be used to describe thunder and lightning, when the air flashes with electricity. Bad weather, with unusually high winds and heavy rain, is also described as a storm. During this type of storm the wind can whirl and twist, whipping sand, dust or water into the air.

In Burkina Faso, a country to the south of the Sahara Desert, violent winds whip up clouds of dust during a storm. The whole sky becomes dark as the air fills with grit and sand.

✳ There are probably about 1600 storms taking place on Earth at any one time.

✳ Other planets have storms as well. Mars is thought to be lashed by sandstorms. Saturn has winds that have been estimated to blow at 1800 kph (1118 mph). According to astronomers, Jupiter has the largest storm of all. It has been whirling around for hundreds of years, and from Earth it looks like an enormous red spot.

The power of the wind

Heavy, cold air presses down upon the surface of the Earth, creating areas of high **air pressure**. But when the Sun heats the land, the air becomes warm and moisture is **evaporated** from the surface. The moisture becomes invisible **water vapour**. The warm air rises quickly and cooler air rushes in to fill the space. The vapour in the rising, cooling air eventually **condenses** to form storm clouds. This is part of a process called **convection**. It occurs all over the world.

There is movement of air between the high pressure areas of the North and South Poles and the low pressure area at the Equator. These constant movements of warm and cold air cause winds. The oceans also play their part in producing winds. During the day, the land heats up more quickly than the sea. This means that the air pressure over the sea is higher than on the land, so that winds blow from the sea to the land. During the night, the land loses its heat more quickly than the sea, the air pressure grows heavier, and the wind blows from the land to the sea.

Wind is the power behind most storms. It drives rain and snow, builds up high waves at sea, and damages buildings. **Meteorologists** are scientists who study the weather. They use a special scale, called the **Beaufort Scale**, to describe wind forces. A completely calm day is Force Zero on the scale. A storm is Force 10. This means that the wind has reached a speed of between 89 and 102 kph (55 and 64 mph). Winds of this speed can blow down trees. A violent storm is Force 11, with winds of between 103 and 117 kph (64 mph and 72 mph). Force 12, with winds of more than 117 kph (73 mph), is called a **hurricane**. At the top of the scale is Force 17, when the wind is racing along at over 200 kph (124 mph).

In most regions, the winds follow a regular pattern. The direction that is most common is said to be that of the "prevailing" wind. The prevailing wind has blown against this tree so often that it is permanently bent sideways.

Whirling winds

The word "hurricane" comes from *hurican,* a word once used by the Carib Indians of the West Indies to describe a "great storm". In the west Pacific, the word **typhoon** is used to describe the same kind of storm. In the Indian Ocean and around Australia, violent winds are called **cyclones**.

Hurricanes form over warm, tropical seas. They are made up of huge spinning wheels of storm clouds, wind and torrential rain. At the centre of the storm is an area of calm, called the **eye**. Between 160 and 240 km (99 and 149 mi) around the eye is a belt of high wind. Near the eye, winds sometimes reach a speed of 180 kph (112 mph). Occasional gusts may even reach 300 kph (186 mph). Winds at the upper and outer edges of a hurricane are less violent.

A tropical hurricane forms a huge spinning mass as it moves across the ocean. At the centre is the calm "eye". Around this blow some of the most violent winds known on Earth.

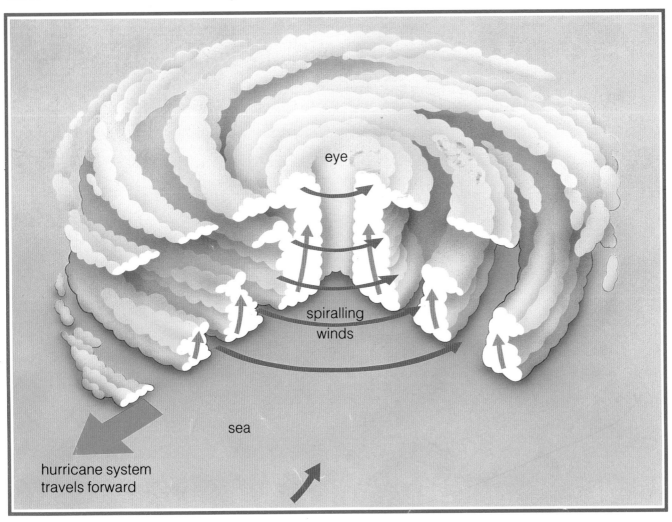

eye

spiralling winds

sea

hurricane system travels forward

Extending upwards by as much as 10 km (6 mi), the hurricane moves across the sea at a speed of up to 90 kph (56 mph). Hurricanes die down when they reach land, but cause extensive damage as they cross islands and coastal areas of the mainland.

An approaching tornado cloud. Tornadoes are so violent that they can lift a house or a train off the ground. They happen so quickly that people are caught unprepared. They can destroy whole towns.

※ In 1987 a waterspout 762 m (2500 ft) high was seen off the English coast.

Twisting and turning

The most violent windstorms of all are called **tornadoes**, twisters or whirlwinds. They are created inside storm clouds during thundery weather. Winds start to spin at speeds of up to 500 kph (311 mph), forming a tight funnel about 100 m (328 ft) wide. The air pressure inside the funnel falls rapidly, and anything in the path of the tornado is sucked up. Tornadoes occur suddenly and die down very quickly.

Sometimes a tornado-like whirlwind will suck up sand in a desert, creating a **dust devil**. It can also suck up water from a sea or large lake, and form a **waterspout**. Waterspouts can be powerful enough to wreck ships.

Danger from wind and water

During a storm, strong winds cause a lot of damage. There is also the added danger of flooding. The wind drives huge waves ashore, flooding coastal areas. Storm winds usually bring heavy rain which causes rivers to break their banks and flood the surrounding land.

This crop was safely harvested, only to be damaged by floods as it lay baled in the fields. A sudden storm caused the nearby river to burst its banks.

Rain is formed because water from oceans, lakes and rivers evaporates when heated by the Sun and turns into an invisible gas called water vapour. The water vapour rises with the warm air. As the air rises, it cools and the vapour condenses, turning into drops of water. These fall to Earth as raindrops, at speeds of up to 30 kph (19 mph). If it is very cold , snow or hail may fall instead of rain. When water falls as rain, snow or hail it is called **precipitation**.

A heavy rainstorm in a town may cause floods because the drains are not big enough to carry away the extra water. In hilly country, a sudden rainstorm can cause a **flash flood**.

Sometimes the amount of water pouring down the hillside starts a landslide. Pieces of land break off and slide downhill, blocking roads and covering buildings.

A severe snowstorm, or **blizzard**, can be just as fierce. The wind whips snow across the landscape, burying it in deep drifts and blocking roads. Hailstorms can be very dangerous indeed. The hailstones sometimes weigh as much as 1 kg (2 lb) each. They can smash glass and even kill people.

A **sandstorm** is caused by strong winds whipping up the fine, desert soil. As the sand settles on the ground, huge banks of sand called dunes form.

Sand from the Sahara Desert fills the air during a storm in the African state of Mali. It becomes hard to breathe, and sand drifts over familiar landmarks.

Thunder and lightning

Thunderstorms are one of the most dangerous of all weather conditions. They begin when huge clouds, up to 15 km (9 mi) high, form in the sky. Warm air inside the cloud rises so quickly that the water vapour in the air cools rapidly and freezes, forming small hailstones. These move up and down inside the clouds, and become electrically charged.

Positive charges of electricity build up at the top of each storm cloud and negative charges build up at the bottom. Then electrical charges may leap down to the ground. They appear as lightning.

When the ground is struck by a charge, a massive current leaps back from the Earth along a channel about 12 mm (0.5 in) wide. The glow from this can be seen as a band several metres thick. When we see the zigzag track of the current clearly, we call it **forked lightning**. Sometimes the light is reflected by cloud over a wide area, and then it is known as **sheet lightning**.

Inside a thundercloud, lightning may pass between the positively charged ice crystals at the top of the cloud, and the negatively charged water droplets at the bottom of the cloud. Lightning can also pass between the cloud and the land.

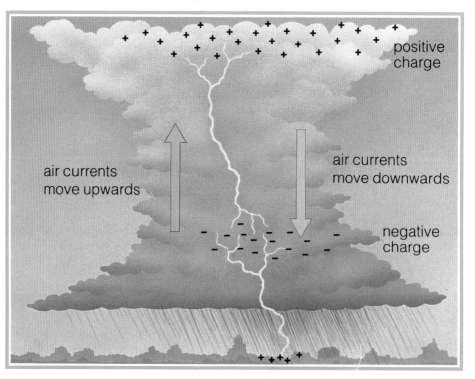

positive charge

air currents move upwards

air currents move downwards

negative charge

Storm clouds gather above Crawney Mountain, in New South Wales, Australia. Most thunderstorms occur in late summer, when warm air loaded with water vapour rises to form huge dark, billowing clouds.

As the electrical current leaps back from the Earth, it may travel as fast as 140,000 km (87,000 mi) a second. It can also reach a temperature of 30,000°C (54,000°F), five times hotter than the surface of the Sun! The heat makes the air around about expand or swell at high speed, causing a shock wave. This makes the booming noise called thunder.

Flash, bang, wallop!

Lightning and thunder happen at exactly the same time, but you see the lightning before you hear the thunder because light travels faster than sound. You can work out how far away the thunderstorm is like this:

As soon as you see the lightning, start counting the seconds. Stop when you hear the thunder, and divide the number you have counted by three. The answer you get tells you roughly how far you are, in kilometres, from the thunderstorm.

✳ The longest lightning flash on record measured over 30 km (19 mi).

Storm zones

The Indian and western Pacific Oceans often experience fierce typhoons and cyclones. The western Atlantic, the Caribbean and the Gulf of Mexico lie on a path followed frequently by violent hurricanes. Most of the worst tornadoes occur in central North America.

The weather conditions in a particular country or place usually follow a pattern over the years, and this is called its **climate**. Places with a hot, tropical climate have the most storms.

Find the cross line, or **latitude**, for the Equator on a world map. The tropics lie about 23.5 degrees north and south of the Equator. Thunderstorms are common near the Equator, because the Sun heats the land intensely in the morning, causing thunderstorms in the late afternoon. Many storms in the middle latitudes are caused by depressions. They form when warm air from subtropical areas meets cold polar air.

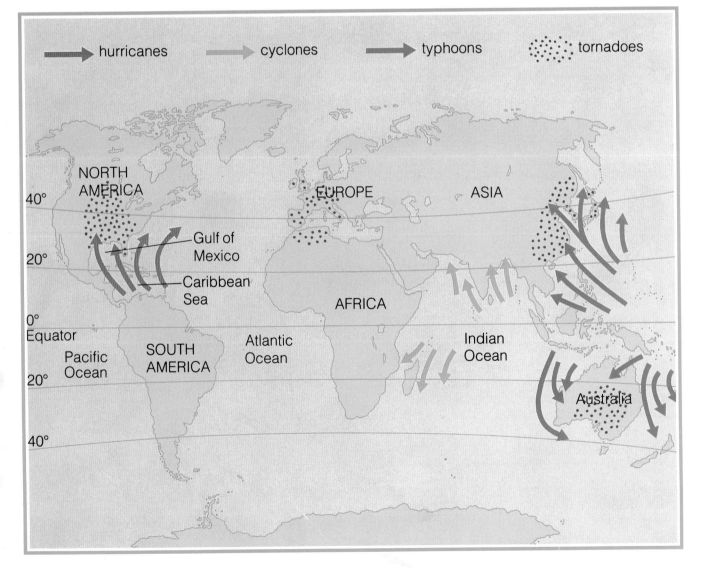

Rain drenches the city streets of Pinang, Malaysia. Each summer the monsoon winds sweep across southern Asia from the ocean. The heavy rains they bring are welcomed by farmers but in the cities they may cause dangerous flooding.

✳ Some of the world's stormiest seas lie below the latitude of 40° south. Sailors call this region the "Roaring Forties".

✳ Thunder is never heard in the icy polar regions. This is because it is so bitterly cold there that storm clouds cannot form.

The rainstorms are coming

In some tropical countries, the heat builds up over several months each year and during this dry season the land becomes warmer and warmer. The air heats up and rises, and colder air full of water vapour rushes in from the ocean. When mountain ranges force this moist air to rise, a wet season begins, with rainy winds called **monsoons**.

15

An eye on the sky

Storms have always been a time of danger for people. In the days when sailing ships crossed the oceans, sailors needed to know when storms were due, so that they could take down their sails. A strong wind could drive the ship on to rocks, or crack the mast, leaving the ship drifting helplessly.

> Mackerel sky and mares' tails
> Make tall ships carry low sails

ran one old saying. Sailors learned to "read" the sky, looking for cloud patterns which would tell them what sort of weather to expect.

A hundred years ago shipwrecks were very common. Sailing vessels were at the mercy of the storm and wind. Today's ships have powerful engines but even so they may sink during a severe storm.

Today pilots of large planes avoid a storm if it is possible, and small planes land at the nearest airport or do not take off at all when stormy weather is forecast. In very windy weather, the drivers of high-sided vehicles avoid crossing suspension bridges and may pull off the road altogether.

Clouds and wind

Weather watchers take note. Towering cumulo-nimbus clouds may bring violent storms, thunder and lightning. The huge mushroom shaped clouds can reach a height of 12 km (7 mi) or more.

Cloud formations are still important to weather forecasters. A low dense blanket of cloud called nimbo-stratus may warn of heavy rain or snow. If the clouds start to race across the sky, a storm is probably on the way. On hot days, when puffy clouds start to form in high, towering columns, called cumulo-nimbus, weather forecasters issue serious storm warnings. Cumulo-nimbus clouds bring rain and thunder.

Recording the weather

Today there are **weather stations** all around the world. Some are in cities, others are on board ships and planes. Every few hours, meteorologists take accurate measurements of the weather conditions. Different instruments are used to take the various measurements. A **barometer** records the air pressure. If this drops very quickly, it means that a storm is on the way, because moist air may be moving into the area at high speed. **Rain gauges** measure the depth of rain that falls, and **anemometers** measure the speed of the wind.

This picture was beamed back to Earth by satellite. It shows Hurricane Allen moving across the Gulf of Mexico, and another hurricane developing off the west coast of the USA. The use of satellite pictures helps meteorologists track the progress of storms and issue advance warnings.

Meteorologists send up instruments in balloons to take measurements of the weather 20 km (12 mi) above the ground. The information is radioed back before the balloon bursts and the instruments return to Earth. Weather **satellites** circle the Earth, sending back computer pictures of the cloud patterns below. On these pictures, hurricanes look like great whirling wheels as they move across the oceans.

Forecasts and warnings

Coastguards keep a constant check on the coastline, watching for ships in trouble and helping to organize rescue attempts in stormy weather. At this coastguard station, a southerly gale warning has been raised on the mast. Sailors know that they must remain in port until the weather clears.

The weather forecasters prepare charts of the weather patterns from all the information that has been collected. They examine the changes that have taken place and use their judgement and special knowledge to make a forecast. Warnings of dangerous weather conditions are broadcast on radio and television. Sailors and pilots are given detailed information about where to expect high winds or storms.

The coastguards control the movement of shipping along the coast. They hoist warning signals on a mast outside the coastguard station to show sailors that a gale is forecast. For example, an upright black cone means a northerly gale. Upside down, it means a southerly gale.

In tropical storm zones, special centres have been set up to track the paths of hurricanes and typhoons, so that meteorologists can try to work out the way a storm will go. When it is clear that a particular area is at risk, they warn people to leave. Every hurricane has its own name. The first hurricane of the season is given a name beginning with A, the second with a B and so on through the hurricane season. The meteorologists once used only female names, but now they use male names as well.

Track the storm

Hurricanes cause a lot of damage, so newspapers often carry reports about them. Check the paper for a hurricane story. What name was given to the hurricane? Where did it do most damage? Find the place in an atlas. Try writing your own newspaper report. It can be either factual or dramatic.

After the storm has passed, the destruction can be seen.

Storms and nature

Much of the Earth's landscape has been shaped by storms over many millions of years. In some places, rough seas have broken down the coastline. Elsewhere, strong winds have uprooted plants so that the soil has turned to fine dust, grit or sand. The wind has then hurled this against rocks to wear them down in their turn. The way in which wind and water wear down the landscape is called **erosion**.

Lightning also affects the natural world. It can burn grass and other plants, split open trees and start forest fires. Lightning can even melt sand, forming glassy lumps called fulgurites.

Waves crash over the rocky shores of the Isle of Islay, as the storm gathers force. The Hebrides, off the western coast of Scotland, bear the full brunt of Atlantic gales.

Coconut palms have springy trunks, which bend when a hurricane blows.

Plants and animals

Plants have developed many ways of protecting themselves against storms. Some grow with their leaves flat against the ground, others anchor themselves with wide-spreading roots. The redwood trees of North America have bark made of a thick, spongy fibre which protects the trunk from lightning fires.

Wild animals often die if they cannot find shelter in a storm. They can also be stranded by floods or forest fires. Birds are sometimes blown thousands of kilometres off course.

However, there are some birds that prefer stormy weather. Storm petrels flutter over the huge waves of the Atlantic Ocean as they search for food, and albatrosses use the gales of the Roaring Forties to help them on long flights around the Southern Ocean.

Lightning starts forest fires in many parts of the world. Birds and animals are driven from their homes by fierce flames and dense smoke. Many animals are killed.

Storm damage

After a bad storm, go out with a notebook and pencil and record any damage the storm has done, especially to plants and animals.

1 Have any trees been uprooted? Try to find out what type of trees they are. How deep did the roots go?

2 Are there broken branches on the ground? Did they cause any damage to anything else as they crashed down?

3 Have any birds' nests been blown or washed out of hedges and trees?

4 Have any plants been covered by floodwater (or even deep puddles)?

5 Has wildlife been disturbed? (For example, have any burrows been flooded?)

6 If the trees were in flower, are there any flowers left?

7 If it is autumn, are there any fruits or leaves left on the trees?

8 Are there any brown patches of grass where lightning has struck?

Storms and people

Severe storms kill and injure people in a number of ways. Trees are sometimes blown down on to cars, trapping and killing the people inside. People may be swept away and drowned by floods. Blizzards and sandstorms are just as dangerous. They change the appearance of the landscape, burying landmarks in drifting snow or sand so that travellers lose their way.

When a storm warning is broadcast on the radio or television, preparations have to be made quickly. In coastal areas, boats are taken out of the water and, where possible, harbour entrances are sealed off against the sea. Around the town, loose objects of all kinds have to be tied down or put away. Plants need protecting or tying to stakes. Pets must be brought indoors. Torches have to be easy to find in case the electricity fails.

When the storm is likely to be very bad, the fire service and other emergency services check the streets, warning people in the area.

At Dhaka, the capital of Bangladesh, survivors of a flood try to keep dry until the water goes down.

Always be prepared for stormy weather when hiking cross-country. Weather forecasts are normally displayed at mountain centres and hostels. Read them carefully. If the forecast is bad, stay at home - even if the weather seems to be fine at the time.

Near rivers or the sea, they often supply sandbags to protect property from floodwater. If the danger is not too serious, they will ask people to stay indoors. If the danger is more serious, people may be asked to leave the area likely to be affected by the storm. This must be properly organized, because if everybody tried to leave in a hurry they could cause traffic jams and widespread panic.

Out in the country

Since weather conditions can change very quickly, walkers and rock-climbers have to be ready for storms even if they start out in fine weather. Warm and waterproof clothing is essential. So are strong footwear, and packs containing maps, torches, whistles, emergency food supplies and flasks of warm drinks. The best plan is to have an experienced group leader in charge of the expedition. He or she will check on local forecasts and the equipment required and make sure that other people know the route that is to be taken.

If a thunderstorm threatens and shelter is needed, it is safer to find a place well away from trees, which are sometimes struck by lightning.

Storm protection

Towns and cities can be badly damaged by storms. Strong winds can lift the roofs off houses, or destroy buildings completely. In desert areas, houses can be buried by sand during sandstorms. Today, structures like bridges and skyscrapers can be tested before they are built. Engineers test the designs on computers and in wind tunnels to see if their structure needs to be strengthened or made more flexible.

Some storm protection ideas have been taken from nature. The tops of skyscrapers are designed to sway slightly in a high wind, just as the trunks of palm trees bend in a hurricane. Skyscrapers are also anchored to the ground with long tubes of steel or concrete. These piles are driven deep into the ground and act as "roots" for the building. Both walls and roofs of buildings in storm zones are now specially strengthened. For example, the John Hancock Centre in Chicago in the USA has huge cross-braces attached to the sides of the building. These braces help the skyscraper withstand the force of high winds.

In 1953 terrible storms flooded the coasts of England and the Netherlands. Trucks, ambulances, boats and buses were used to evacuate Canvey Island, one of the worst hit areas of England's east coast. Afterwards it was decided to build new coastal defences.

The Thames Barrier was opened in 1984. It protects the people of London from floods. If exceptionally high tides surge up the river, 20 metre-high (66 ft) steel gates close to protect the city. The Dutch coast is protected by the dams and barriers of the Delta Project which opened in 1986.

Tall buildings are fitted with lightning conductors to carry lightning safely to the ground. They are also often fitted with anemometers to record the wind speed at roof level. This information is useful to designers when they plan new buildings in a city.

Since floodwater needs to drain away quickly, many cities have huge storm drains to carry away rushing water. In coastal towns, sea walls and dykes are built to keep out waves. To prevent rivers bursting their banks, walls or embankments are sometimes raised. In the USA these are called levees. Levees stretch along the Mississippi-Missouri river system for over 2700 km (1600 mi). Special flood barriers have been built in some large cities to protect them from the water that sometimes surges upriver during storms.

A stormy future?

In recent years many parts of the world have experienced an increase in the number of severe storms. This may be part of a normal long-term weather pattern, or it may be the first signs of global warming. The main cause of global warming is the gases given out by factories and vehicles which have increased the level of carbon dioxide in the air around the Earth, trapping heat in the lower atmosphere. The situation has been made worse by the destruction of the world's rain forests, which help to balance the planet's levels of carbon dioxide. Some scientists claim that by the year 2050, the Earth may be hotter than at any time during the last 100,000 years.

In October 1987, high winds devastated large areas of southern England and northern France. Ancient woodland was destroyed and many strong tree trunks were split like matchwood.

In 1988, severe flooding of the Nile River spread to Khartoum, the capital of Sudan. The city was already full of refugees from war and famine. Flooding may become increasingly common if global warming continues.

If global warming does continue, crops will be destroyed by severe storms and the polar ice caps may melt, causing sea levels to rise. This would affect all low-lying land not protected by flood barriers and sea defences. Areas such as Florida Keys, in the USA, or the land around the mouths of the Nile River in Egypt, or the Ganges River in Bangladesh and India may be completely flooded.

What can be done

If global warming continues, scientists have put forward some fantastic ideas to help counter its effects. They have suggested building a vast sunshade in space, and painting the deserts white to help the Earth reflect the Sun's heat. Algae could be grown on marine farms to help absorb carbon dioxide.

Such measures may prove unnecessary. In the meantime, we must stop the destruction of the rain forests, burn less fuel and ensure that factories and power stations are cleaner.

Glossary

air pressure   The force with which the air presses against the Earth's surface at any point. Areas of low pressure are sometimes called depressions, and bring storms. Areas of high pressure are called anticyclones, and bring fine weather.

anemometer   An instrument used to measure the speed of the wind.

atmosphere   The mixture of gases, such as oxygen and nitrogen, which make up the air around our planet.

barometer   An instrument used to measure air pressure.

Beaufort Scale   A listing of wind strengths in order of severity from zero to seventeen. It was invented in 1805 by a British admiral called Sir Francis Beaufort.

blizzard   A violent windy snowstorm.

climate   The average weather conditions of a region over a long period.

condense   To become more dense. When vapour condenses, it turns into a liquid.

convection   A circulation of the air caused when air rises and is replaced by falling, cooler air.

cyclone   1. A hurricane-force wind or typhoon.
2. Any area of low pressure, a depression.

dust devil   A column of swirling dust or sand raised into the air by a small whirlwind.

erosion   The process by which rock and soil are worn away by wind and water.

evaporate   To turn into vapour.

eye   The calm area at the centre of a hurricane.

flash flood   A short but heavy flood.

forked lightning   A jagged, forking streak of light caused by an electric current passing through a cloud, or from a cloud to the ground.

hurricane   A violent, whirling storm common in tropical regions, in which winds reach Force 12 on the Beaufort Scale.

latitude   One of the imaginary lines drawn horizontally around the world on a map or globe. The vertical lines show longitude. Together they are used to locate a point on the map.

meteorologist   Someone who studies meteorology, or the science of weather conditions.

monsoon   A seasonal wind, like those of southern Asia. The south-west monsoon blows in the summer season, bringing heavy rainstorms.

precipitation   Deposits of water, either liquid or solid, that come from the atmosphere, including rain, snow, sleet, hail, dew or frost.

rain gauge   An instrument used to measure the amount of rainfall.

sandstorm   A high wind which picks up particles of sand from desert areas.

satellite   A spacecraft which circles a planet. Weather satellites send back pictures of cloud patterns and take measurements of conditions in the atmosphere.

sheet lightning   A widely spread flash of light caused when clouds reflect lightning.

storm   A limited period of violent weather conditions, marked by high wind, rain, snow, hail, thunder or lightning.

tornado   A narrow but very violent whirlwind which can lift objects as heavy as houses or trains into the air.

typhoon   A word used to describe hurricane-force winds in the South China Sea and North Pacific.

waterspout   A tall column of water created when a whirlwind occurs over a lake or sea.

water vapour   An invisible gas in the air. Water becomes vapour when it dries out, or evaporates.

weather station   A base where scientists take accurate measurements of daily weather conditions.

Index